A BIBLE GUIDE TO OVERCOMING ADDICTION

Stephen D. Baker, M.Min

CrossLife Press

Copyright © 2020 Stephen D. Baker

All rights reserved

The characters and events portrayed in this book are fictitious. Any similarity to real persons, living or dead, is coincidental and not intended by the author.

No part of this book may be reproduced, or stored in a retrieval system, or transmitted in any form or by any means, electronic, mechanical, photocopying, recording, or otherwise, without express written permission of the publisher.

All Scripture Quotations are from the Authorized King James Version of the Bible. In the United States the KJV is in the public domain. In the United Kingdom, rights are vested in the Crown.

ISBN-13: 9798574060933

Cover Photo: 135021534 © Tom Wang | Dreamstime.com
Printed in the United States of America

*TO EVERYONE WHO HAS STRUGGLED AND OVERCOME.
TO THOSE WHO HAVEN'T OVERCOME YET, BUT WILL.*

CONTENTS

Title Page
Copyright
Dedication
INTRODUCTION   1
Part 1. INTRODUCTORY THOUGHTS   3
1. DOES THE BIBLE TALK ABOUT ADDICTION?   4
2. UNDERSTANDING THE POWER OF ADDICTION   6
3. UNDERSTANDING THE DECEPTION OF ADDICTION   12
Part 2. BIBLICAL/SCIENTIFIC APPROACH   18
4. UNDERSTANDING ADDICTION USING A SCIENTIFIC APPROACH: THE ABC CHART.   19
5. UNDERSTANDING AND DEALING WITH TRIGGERS FROM A BIBLICAL PERSPECTIVE   30
6. UNDERSTANDING OUR SIN NATURE.   41
PART 3. BIBLICAL IDEAS TO DEFEAT ADDICTION   46
7. UNDERSTANDING THE BIBLICAL IDEA OF REPLACEMENT.   47
8. UNDERSTANDING HOW TO KNOW, RECKON, AND YIELD.   54
9. UNDERSTANDING LIFE IN THE SPIRIT.   58
10. UNDERSTANDING THE IMPORTANCE OF CHRISTIAN FELLOWSHIP.   63

11. CLOSING THOUGHTS.	67
About The Author	69
Bibliography	71
Books By This Author	73
Legal Things You Should Know.	75

INTRODUCTION

The human mind is powerful. What we think and believe determines what solutions we use to handle difficulties. People find themselves dependent on alcohol, prescription drugs, illegal drugs, gambling, pornography, social media, and all sorts of other things to get through life. Does the Bible have anything to say about the phenomenon we call addiction? Indeed, it does. Does the Bible offer a solution? Again, it does. We will examine a Biblical way to overcome addictions in this book.

Are these strategies evidence-based? Absolutely. The Bible is thousands of years old and has changed many millions of lives. There are countless testimonies of alcoholics who have become sober, drug addicts who have quit drugs, prostitutes who have become pure, and sinners who have become saints. Much of the New Testament was written by a man named the Apostle Paul. Before he met Jesus Christ and became a Christian, Paul hunted down, jailed, and persecuted believers. He said, "This is a faithful saying, and worthy of all acceptation, that Christ Jesus came into the world to save sinners; of whom I am chief." (1 Timothy 1:15) Paul called himself "The Chief of Sinners" yet God saved him. If God could change Paul's life, He can change your life too!

Does the Bible give a specific formula of rules or methods for overcoming addiction? It does not. The Bible is not a book of science, medicine, or psychology. While it speaks about these things, the Bible is primarily a spiritual book about man's relationship with God through Jesus Christ. There is no Step 1., Step 2., Step 3., formula given in Scripture. But the Bible talks about addiction and gives some general principles that can be used in fighting it. Surprisingly, many of these principles harmonize with modern thought on addiction treatment found in scientific methods such as Cognitive Behavioral Therapy (CBT).[1]

You do not have to live another moment in bondage to addiction. The Bible has the solution!

PART 1. INTRODUCTORY THOUGHTS

ADDICTION IN PROVERBS; ITS POWER & DECEPTION.

1. DOES THE BIBLE TALK ABOUT ADDICTION?

Did addiction exist when the Bible was written, or is it a modern phenomenon? It turns out that addiction is as ancient as mankind. In the book of Proverbs, the wisest man who ever lived, King Solomon, wrote the following:

"Who hath woe? who hath sorrow? who hath contentions? who hath babbling? who hath wounds without cause? who hath redness of eyes? They that tarry long at the wine; they that go to seek mixed wine. Look not thou upon the wine when it is red, when it giveth his colour in the cup, when it moveth itself aright. At the last it biteth like a serpent, and stingeth like an adder. Thine eyes shall behold strange women, and thine heart shall utter perverse things. Yea, thou shalt be as he that lieth down in the midst of the sea, or as he that lieth upon the top of a mast. They have stricken me, shalt thou say, and I was not sick; they have beaten me, and I felt it not: when shall I awake? I will seek it yet again." (Proverbs 23:29-35)

"A PATTERN THEY CANNOT SEEM TO QUIT, NO MATTER WHAT THE COSTS ARE"

In this illustration, the alcoholic commits fornication, becomes sick and dizzy, gets beat up, passes out, and when he wakes up: he decides to get drunk again! If this does not describe addiction, what does? People with addictions may lose their jobs, wives, husbands, children, cars, credit, and any number of other things.[2] But they keep drinking or using. It is a pattern that they cannot seem to quit, no matter what the costs are!

Does this leave the addicted person with no hope? Absolutely not! In the example of the alcoholic from Proverbs, there is an emphasis that such behavior *can* and *should* be avoided. If it can be avoided, then addiction is not undefeatable or inevitable. However, addiction is powerful! In the next chapter, we will examine a Biblical view of the power of addiction and learn the first steps to overcome it.

2. UNDERSTANDING THE POWER OF ADDICTION

The Apostle Paul spoke of power; the same kind of power that is present in addiction. In a letter to the Church at Corinth, he wrote: "All things are lawful unto me, but all things are not expedient: all things are lawful for me, but I will not be brought under the power of any. Meats for the belly, and the belly for meats: but God shall destroy both it and them. Now the body is not for fornication, but for the Lord; and the Lord for the body." (1 Corinthians 6:12-13)

Fornication was a common practice in the society of the city of Corinth where Paul sent this letter. Not only was sexual sin common, but a part of religion, in which professional temple prostitutes worked to help worshippers carry out their "worship" through sex acts. Fornication in ancient Greek/Roman society also included drawings and writings that we would recognize today as pornography.

Paul wrote to the Corinthian church that while "all things (were) lawful…all things (were) not expedient." (V. 12) The word translated, "expedient" means "to help, be profitable…"[3] In our modern world, many things are lawful that are not helpful. It is legal to drink alcohol and get intoxicated when you are past a certain age. It is legal in some jurisdictions to smoke marijuana for recreational purposes. It is legal in some places to hire a prostitute. It is legal to look at pornography when you are past a certain age.

Yet, none of these things are expedient or helpful or profitable to you in the long run.

However, they may be *very helpful* in the short term to get through whatever problem you are facing. For instance, marijuana is good at making a person feel better. So, if you are experiencing sadness, getting together with some friends and smoking a joint may be helpful. But it is only helpful for the *short term* until you need the next fix.

There is another unfortunate consequence of legal things that are not helpful in the long term: they tend to exercise *power* over you. No one will deny that drugs and alcohol can be very powerful. Even a drug like marijuana, which is not physically addictive, can be powerful enough that it is hard to give up. Pornography can keep a person in powerful bondage for years. What does the Bible say about these things?

Paul wrote: "…I will not be brought under the power of any." (V. 12) The word translated "power" means, "to *control:* - exercise authority upon, bring under the power of."[4] Paul was simply saying, "I will not be controlled by anything. I will not have anything other than Jesus Christ exercise authority over me."

Speaking of *control*, in his book, <u>The Heart of Addiction</u>, psychiatrist and addiction expert, Dr. Lance Dodes, writes about a client named Michael. He says:

> We soon discovered that the moment Michael decided to drink, he had already accomplished something. In making the decision, he had the sense that he had reversed the helplessness he felt…He no longer felt helpless, because he knew at that moment that he could, and would, take an action that would make him feel better.
>
> Once Michael realized this, the emotional purpose of his drinking began to make sense. He had felt driven to drink because he had to get out of his trap. Drinking reversed his helplessness by placing him in control of how he felt (alcohol and drugs in general are particularly apt for this purpose—altering how one feels is just what they do). But he had actually begun to achieve this goal before he had

swallowed a drop. So, although alcohol could change his mood, it was clear that it was the meaning of feeling empowered that was critical here.[5]

It is interesting that Dr. Dodes pinpoints the need to take control of an intolerable situation in which a person feels trapped,[6] as the primary psychological motivator for substance use/abuse. Yet, the Bible teaches that those substances have the opposite effect on the user. While they may give a sense of taking control of one's life, they actually take control *from* the user. Therefore, Paul says: "All things are lawful unto me, but all things are not expedient: all things are lawful for me, but I will not be brought under the power of any." (V. 12)

In the case of the Corinthian believers, fornication could bring them under its power. In our case, it may be fornication and it may be liquor or cigarettes or prescription drugs or internet poker. Whatever it is, we use it to escape, to fill a void, to address a bad feeling, to feel in control. But we end up having more and more power taken from us and yielded to the addiction.

Addictions Can Seem Powerful But That Power Is Limited By The Will Of Man.

Paul wrote, "I will not be brought under the power of any." (V. 12) We learn from this that addictions are not so powerful after all! If something can overcome the will of man, it is very powerful. If the will of man can overcome it, its power is limited. Some think that certain drugs, like nicotine, are so powerfully addictive that smokers are compelled to smoke even when they do not want to anymore because of the negative consequences.[7] But think of what Paul is writing about here.

First, Paul was a single man and he lived in a society where sex was readily available.

Second, there are very few things that are more powerful and compelling than the human sex drive. In fact, for some drugs, one of the chief benefits is that they enhance sex. So what is the driving force in drugs like Ecstasy? The drug itself, or the feeling it gives, a lot of which has to do with sex? It is undeniable that sex is powerful!

Third, fornication was totally legal in Corinth. Paul is not arguing against something that would get the church members arrested. He is arguing against a sinful; yet acceptable part of society. That gave fornication power through social approval.

Understanding these three things, we see how powerful Paul's statement about the human will is: "I will not be brought under the power of any." (V. 12) Powerful addictions, even those we feel compelled to do, can be limited by the power of the will of men and women.

Addictions Are Not As Powerful As They Seem.

That is why *deceit* is necessary for addictions to work. You must be tricked into thinking that a drug or sexual activity, or substance is powerful enough to take care of your problems and too powerful for you to overcome. But again: addictions cannot be all that powerful if Paul was able to say, "I will not be brought under the power of any." (V. 12)

Paul looked at fornication and said, "I won't do it! I won't be brought under its power!" You can do the same thing with any substance or activity. You can say "no!" Believe it or not, you can enjoy life while saying "no!" too.

What About Chemical Effects On The Brain? Aren't Those Powerful And Hard To Overcome?

Someone asks: "Don't drugs affect the brain?" Absolutely, they do! The National Institute on Drug Abuse (NIH) says:

> The feeling of pleasure is how a healthy brain identifies and reinforces beneficial behaviors, such as eating, socializing, and sex. Our brains are wired to increase

the odds that we will repeat pleasurable activities. The neurotransmitter dopamine is central to this. Whenever the reward circuit is activated by a healthy, pleasurable experience, a burst of dopamine signals that something important is happening that needs to be remembered. This dopamine signal causes changes in neural connectivity that make it easier to repeat the activity again and again without thinking about it,[8] leading to the formation of habits.[9]

Just as drugs produce intense euphoria, they also produce much larger surges of dopamine, powerfully reinforcing the connection between consumption of the drug, the resulting pleasure, and all the external cues linked to the experience. Large surges of dopamine "teach" the brain to seek drugs at the expense of other, healthier goals and activities.[10]

"If drugs cause an increase in dopamine, doesn't that make them harder to stop?" Certainly, it is a challenge. However, lots of things increase dopamine. Chocolate, exercise, sex, listening to music; all of these things and many more increase dopamine levels in the brain. The fact that brain chemicals are affected by drugs means less when we think. It certainly does not mean that drugs are so powerful that they cannot be refused. It also does not mean that drugs are so powerful that they cannot be overcome; otherwise, no one would ever stop using them!

We know that alcohol affects the brain, yet the Bible gives hope to alcoholics. Paul wrote: "Nor thieves, nor covetous, nor drunkards, nor revilers, nor extortioners, shall inherit the kingdom of God. And such were some of you: but ye are washed, but ye are sanctified, but ye are justified in the name of the Lord Jesus, and by the Spirit of our God." (1 Corinthians 6:10-11) Some of the Corinthians were drunks before they met Jesus Christ. Yet, they had been set free and now, they were living a different kind of life.

Because of chemical changes in the brain caused by long-term drug/alcohol abuse, it may be necessary, under professional care, to enter a detox/rehab facility. My own experience in dealing with teens who need to detox is that after a few days, they begin to think normally again and can receive help from counseling. If people who lived long before drug rehab, A.A., and many other services that we have available today could be set free from the bondage of chemical addiction, so can you!

The bottom line is this: drugs are NOT so powerful and permanently mind-altering that they cannot be overcome by the power of God and the will of man. We will examine this further in the next chapter.

3. UNDERSTANDING THE DECEPTION OF ADDICTION

The book of James teaches a lot of very helpful things about temptation. As we have learned, addiction can be either authorized or stopped by the will of man and as we will see, mankind's will is influenced by temptation. Because of this, it will be helpful to examine a way to understand and deal with temptation. James wrote:

"Let no man say when he is tempted, I am tempted of God: for God cannot be tempted with evil, neither tempteth he any man: But every man is tempted, when he is drawn away of his own lust, and enticed. Then when lust hath conceived, it bringeth forth sin: and sin, when it is finished, bringeth forth death. Do not err, my beloved brethren. Every good gift and every perfect gift is from above, and cometh down from the Father of lights, with whom is no variableness, neither shadow of turning. Of his own will begat he us with the word of truth, that we should be a kind of firstfruits of his creatures." (James 1:13-18)

In looking at this passage of Scripture, we note these four things:

1. All addiction works through temptation and triggers.
2. God does not tempt us to evil.

3. We tempt ourselves through deception + consent of the will.

4. God has good things that will satisfy the needs we try to satisfy through sin.

Now let us examine each of these things in detail:

All Addiction Works Through Temptation And Triggers.

Addiction is caused by *something*, and that *something* is commonly referred to as a *trigger*. We will examine triggers later in this book, but for now, triggers are *events that cause us to want to give in to our addictive behavior*.

Temptation is discussed by James and we will examine it now. Temptation is *a deceitful desire for something that is forbidden by Scripture*. In other words, temptation leads to sin, and sin is defined in the Bible as disobedience to God's law. "Whosoever committeth sin transgresseth also the law: for sin is the transgression of the law." (1 John 3:4)

So, temptation is when we desire to do something that goes against God's law. A good example would be fornication. While fornication, in many circumstances, is perfectly legal; it is forbidden in Scripture. "Flee fornication. Every sin that a man doeth is without the body; but he that committeth fornication sinneth against his own body." (1 Corinthians 6:18) So, a man may be tempted to look at pornography or have sex outside of marriage. These are examples of fornication (a word that includes all kinds of sexual sins). Temptation is simply a desire for something like this that is forbidden by Scripture.

Other examples of things forbidden by Scripture that we may be tempted to do are:

1. Drunkenness: "And be not drunk with wine, wherein is excess; but be filled with the Spirit;" (Ephesians 5:18)

2. Drug Use: "Now the works of the flesh are manifest,

which are these; Adultery, fornication, uncleanness, lasciviousness, Idolatry, <u>witchcraft</u>, hatred, variance, emulations, wrath, strife, seditions, heresies, Envyings, murders, drunkenness, revellings, and such like: of the which I tell you before, as I have also told you in time past, that they which do such things shall not inherit the kingdom of God." (Galatians 5:19-21) In this example, the word translated "witchcraft" is associated with the administering of drugs. In other words, a person might use mind-altering drugs as a method of "casting-spells." This is exactly what illegal drugs do today. Do you need to calm down? Take this drug. Do you need energy? Take this drug. Do you need to have fun? Take this drug and see amazing things! Drugs cast plenty of spells on their users.
3. Gluttony: "For the drunkard and the glutton shall come to poverty: and drowsiness shall clothe a man with rags." (Proverbs 23:21)

God Does Not Tempt Us To Do Evil.

The Bible says, "Let no man say when he is tempted, I am tempted of God: for God cannot be tempted with evil, neither tempteth he any man: But every man is tempted, when he is drawn away of his own lust, and enticed." (James 1:13, 14)

God never tempts us to do wrong. I knew an associate pastor who left his wife for the church secretary in an adulterous affair. He said, "God has brought us together!" Of course, we all know that is ridiculous! But think of the things that people attribute to God that have nothing to do with God. In the Garden of Eden, Adam blamed God for giving him Eve who offered him the forbidden fruit which he decided to eat. "And the man said, The woman whom thou gavest to be with me, she gave me of the tree, and I did eat." (Genesis 3:12)

It does not help to blame God (or anyone else for that matter) for the temptation that you may experience to drink, do drugs, gamble, etc. Blaming others is an easy thing to do because it helps you to feel that you are not that bad of a person and it gives you an excuse for not changing.

For many years, I stayed in a situation that I should have gotten out of but was afraid to leave. My wife begged me to leave, but I stayed. It was easy to stay and blame the people who were present in that situation for why I could not move forward in life. But the truth was, the problem was not them. It was me and the fact that I chose not to leave that situation. It was not God's fault that Adam ate the forbidden fruit nor was it Eve's fault. Adam could have said, "No!" But he did not. It does not help to blame God or others for temptation.

We Tempt Ourselves Through Deception + Consent Of The Will.

What could be worse than self-deception? Yet, that is exactly what the Bible talks about here. "But every man is tempted, when he is drawn away of his own lust, and enticed." (James 1:14) In this verse, "drawn away" means, as a figure of speech to, "...lure forth: in hunting and fishing as game is lured from its hiding place, so man by lure is allured from the safety of self-restraint to sin."[11]

The illustration of hunting or fishing is used to describe how we are tempted. When I go fishing, I do not go to the water and start yelling, "Hey fish! I'm here to catch and eat you!" No. I trick the fish. I cast a lure in the water that looks like a worm or bug or something the fish will like. I wait for the fish to bite. Then, the fish is hooked!

The interesting thing is that deceitful temptation takes place through our "own lusts" (V. 14) Our sinful nature tricks us into taking the bait. There is something inside that pulls us in the wrong direction. That is indwelling sin. The Apostle Paul said, "Now then it is no more I that do it, but sin that dwelleth in me." (Romans 7:17) Paul recognized what is true for all believers. All of us have a "sin nature," also called "the old man" and "indwelling sin." This sinfulness pushes us in the wrong direction, but we can resist it!

As a believer in Jesus Christ, I can say "no" to indwelling sin. I do not have to be deceived and take the bait.

The only way I will take the bait is if I *consent* to do the thing I am being tempted to do. The Bible says, "Then when lust hath conceived, it bringeth forth sin: and sin, when it is finished, bringeth forth death." (James 1:15) Lust must conceive for sin to be brought forth.

A beautiful moment has arrived! A baby is born! But this baby does not look cute or cuddly. It is an awful, hideous, angry little monster. Lust (a desire to do wrong) has had a baby, and that baby is sin! How does lust conceive? How does temptation become sin? The answer is that you and I must *consent* to give in to the temptation. We must quit resisting and start complying.

Here is the interesting thing about that: because complying feels like taking an action, psychologically, it can give us a feeling of relief from the pressures we are experiencing.

For example, a man hates his job, but he is under pressure from his family to keep it because they need the money. He comes home every night and drinks alcohol until he is drunk. His wife is very angry because he does this. Why does he do it?

Because he does not believe that he can quit the job which he hates, temptation tricks him into doing the one thing he can do to escape: getting wasted on alcohol. Of course, this is not really an escape. It is bondage. "Then when lust hath conceived, it bringeth forth sin: and sin, when it is finished, bringeth forth death." (James 1:15)

It is also not the *one thing* that he can do. There may be several choices before him, like getting a different or better job or taking some classes so that he might be eligible for a promotion. But at the time, he feels like this is his only choice. That is part of the deception of temptation. Unfortunately, that deception is self-deception.

God Has Good Things That Will Satisfy The Needs We Try To Satisfy Through Sin.

James goes on to say, "Do not err, my beloved brethren. Every good gift and every perfect gift is from above, and cometh down from the Father of lights, with whom is no variableness, neither shadow of turning." (James 1:16-17) God has good gifts for us. It is a lie of the Devil that God wants us to be miserable. Satan used this lie with Eve in the Garden of Eden.

"But of the fruit of the tree which is in the midst of the garden, God hath said, Ye shall not eat of it, neither shall ye touch it, lest ye die. And the serpent said unto the woman, Ye shall not surely die: For God doth know that in the day ye eat thereof, then your eyes shall be opened, and ye shall be as gods, knowing good and evil." (Genesis 3:3-5)

Satan said, "God doesn't want you to eat the forbidden fruit because He knows that you will have a better life if you do! You will be like Him! God is keeping you from that!" The same lies are used today: "God doesn't want you to be happy. He wants you to stay in this job/church/relationship where you are miserable. There is no chance for you to improve the situation or find anything better so why not do the only thing you can do: give into your addiction!"

However, the Bible teaches that God has good and perfect gifts for us that will satisfy our needs. "Do not err, my beloved brethren. Every good gift and every perfect gift is from above, and cometh down from the Father of lights, with whom is no variableness, neither shadow of turning." (James 1:16-17) If we seek God's will and take advantage of these good gifts, then we will not feel trapped in a hopeless situation that makes us feel as if our only choice is to give in to temptation.

In the next chapter, we will look at a scientific approach that will help us to determine our triggers, and also learn how to challenge false beliefs that lead to giving in to temptation.

PART 2. BIBLICAL/ SCIENTIFIC APPROACH

ABC CHART, THOUGHT STOPPING, TRIGGERS, SIN & STRUGGLE.

4. UNDERSTANDING ADDICTION USING A SCIENTIFIC APPROACH: THE ABC CHART.

The Bible is not a book *about* science. It is also not an anti-science book. The Bible is only *opposed* to *fake science*: "O Timothy, keep that which is committed to thy trust, avoiding profane and vain babblings, and oppositions of science falsely so called:" (1 Timothy 6:20) The Bible never stands in opposition to real scientific discovery.

Through advances in the scientific treatment of addictions in the field of psychology, tools have been developed to help people suffering from dependency disorders to work through their problems and find solutions.

We will use one of these tools, modified for our purposes, and show how it relates to the Bible. This tool is the ABC Chart. Here is how it works:

A. Stands for Activating Event. This is the trigger event that caused the person to decide to give in to their addiction.

B. Stands for Beliefs. Any time a person gives in to their addiction, certain false beliefs are involved. This is where the self-deception that we studied in the book of James comes in. A person tricks himself or herself into believing that giving in to the temptation is a good idea. One of the keys to using an ABC Chart is to challenge these false beliefs.

C. Stands for Consequences. These are the results (usually bad) of giving in to the addiction.

Now, we will look at a historical scenario and complete an ABC Chart to see how it can be used. Here is the scenario, taken from the Old Testament book of 2 Samuel:

"And it came to pass, after the year was expired, at the time when kings go forth to battle, that David sent Joab, and his servants with him, and all Israel; and they destroyed the children of Ammon, and besieged Rabbah. But David tarried still at Jerusalem. And it came to pass in an eveningtide, that David arose from off his bed, and walked upon the roof of the king's house: and from the roof he saw a woman washing herself; and the woman was very beautiful to look upon. And David sent and enquired after the woman. And one said, Is not this Bathsheba, the daughter of Eliam, the wife of Uriah the Hittite? And David sent messengers, and took her; and she came in unto him, and he lay with her; for she was purified from her uncleanness: and she returned unto her house. And the woman conceived, and sent and told David, and said, I am with child." (2 Samuel 11:1-5)

King David ends up having sex with another man's wife and she becomes pregnant. If we were to read on, we would discover that because he could not cover the indiscretion up, he ended up having her husband killed. Then, he married her. However, his sin was eventually discovered and punished.

Despite this horrible incident, David is shown in the Bible to be a good man and a heroic figure in the life of the Nation of Israel. Why did something like this happen to an otherwise good man? Let us use our imaginations and an ABC Chart to figure it out. In this case, we will do the A first, then the C and finally the B.

As we do this, we will use our imaginations to explore David's beliefs at the time. If you are making a chart about yourself and reflecting on an addictive episode in your own life, you will identify your own beliefs, determine what was true and what was false, and challenge any false beliefs.

❉ ❉ ❉

Activating Events:

1. David stays home when other kings go to war.
2. David walks on his roof sometime after 3 p.m. He is looking down. It probably was not unusual for people to bathe in their gardens or open spaces that could be seen from the King's Palace.
3. David sees a beautiful woman bathing.

Consequences:

1. David gets Bathsheba pregnant.
2. David tries to cover it up and ends up committing murder.
3. David tries to cover this up and ends up being exposed.
4. David loses fellowship with God and must repent.
5. David suffers long-term consequences for his actions.

Beliefs:

1. David thinks: "I don't need to go out to battle like other kings. I have people that can take care of that." (Maybe David was depressed at the time?)
2. David thinks: "I will take a walk on the roof and get some fresh air. Maybe there will be some hot looking babe taking a bath. That would be nice!" (Maybe David's marriage isn't going all that well.)
3. David thinks: "Wow! That woman is gorgeous! I am the king, and I can have her come to the palace and meet me. My wife is always critical of me anyway. She doesn't appreciate me."

4. David thinks: "I can have sex with her, and she probably won't get pregnant anyway."

* * *

Now, let us challenge these beliefs:

* * *

False Belief:

"I don't need to go out to battle like other kings. I have people that can take care of that."

Challenge:

"I am the leader of Israel. Even if I do not feel like going to battle, it is my job to do so. I should go."

False Belief:

"I will take a walk on the roof and get some fresh air. Maybe there will be some hot looking babe taking a bath. That would be nice!"

Challenge:

"It's not a good idea for me to go out on the roof and start looking. I am married. Things aren't going well, and I am in a vulnerable situation. I am liable to sin. I owe it to God not to do this. I have too many good things to fall for something like this."

False Belief:

"Wow! That woman is gorgeous! I am the king, and I can have her come to the palace and meet me. My wife is always critical of me anyway. She doesn't appreciate me."

Challenge:

"Even though I am the king, God is the King of Kings who appointed me as King of Israel. God wouldn't want me to do this even though my wife is critical. Maybe my wife and I can get some help from Nathan (the prophet). I should not do this!"

False Belief:

"I can have sex with this woman and she probably won't get pregnant anyway."

Challenge:

"This is a huge risk! Even if we take precautions, she could still get pregnant and then what? What will God think of this? I know He doesn't want me to do it!"

※ ※ ※

From this, you can see how the ABC Chart works. Now, let us study each part in detail:

Activating Event

This is the trigger that starts the thought process that leads to giving into temptation. Triggers can be something as simple as a habitual situation. For instance: Every Friday night after work, James goes to the pub with some of his friends. He gets drunk and comes home drunk, upsetting his wife and children. In this case, his weekly routine is to go to the pub with friends. If he simply gets a new group of friends or quits going to the pub, his activating event will not take place and he will not come home drunk.

Triggers can also be deep-rooted and long-term issues which manifest in different ways.[12] For example: When Sue was a child, she was criticized constantly by her mother for being overweight. She began to feel that she could never please her mother, so she started eating more and gaining more weight. Now, she is an adult and weighs close to 350 pounds. She constantly criticizes herself for this, feels hopeless and eats ice cream and chocolate bars to make herself feel better. Her husband nags her about losing weight, which upsets her and causes her to binge eat more sweets.

In this case, Sue's triggers are her own self-criticism (learned from her mother's criticism when she was a child), and her husband's criticism (which reminds her of her mother's criticism).

Triggers for alcoholism too may be deep-rooted from childhood. It is not important whether alcoholism is a disease that is inherited (as many believe), or learned behavior (as others contend). The triggers do not change. A man who drinks may have grown up in a home with an alcoholic parent. He saw the parent use drink as a drug to solve depression, financial worries, work worries, etc. He has now learned to use it to cope with his problems.

It may be so connected to the relationship he had with his father or mother that he considers it a part of his own family identity. "We are a family of alcoholics. It is in my genes." When a similar situation happens to him now, (for example he is laid off at work and cannot pay the bills on time), he uses the thing that he is comfortable with to take control of the situation. He drinks alcohol, just like his father did.

Any time you end up having an episode in which you fall for the temptation to give in to your addiction, use the ABC Chart to determine what event activated this process. Remember, that it may be something that is deep-rooted and has been a part of your life for years.

"YOU WOULD DO ANYTHING TO ESCAPE."

Another aspect of triggers is that they may be based on something that happened in the past but is not happening in the present. Because the trigger events are *similar*, they take you back to the horrible things that happened in the past. These are things you would do anything to escape from.

For example years ago, during the "Great Recession," I went through a period of extreme loss. I lost my ministry. I lost financial stability when our family business had to close. I lost my father when he passed away (I had already lost my mother years before). I also went through marriage problems and was afraid I would lose my wife. All of this loss was life-changing and years later, whenever things would start to go wrong, I would think: "Oh no. I am back in the same place I was before. I am going to go through the same things again!"

The truth was, I was nowhere near the place I had been during the "Great Recession." I did not have a father who was going to pass away or a business that was going under. But because events can create a similar sense of desperation as things in the past, these events made me think I was in the same place I had been years before. I had to tell myself, "You are not living through the 'Great Recession' again. You are not going to lose your father again. You are not going to lose everything again. This is not the same."

This is both an example of a trigger, and challenging false beliefs.

Beliefs: True And False

Beliefs are very important. We are saved by faith in Jesus Christ. "For God so loved the world, that he gave his only begotten Son, that whosoever believeth in him should not perish, but have everlasting life. " (John 3:16)

Beliefs impact how we behave: "By faith Noah, being warned of God of things not seen as yet, moved with fear, prepared an ark to the saving of his house; by the which he condemned the world, and became heir of the righteousness which is by faith." (Hebrews 11:7)

Beliefs are demonstrated by works: "Yea, a man may say, Thou hast faith, and I have works: shew me thy faith without thy works, and I will shew thee my faith by my works." (James 2:18)

Knowing these things, it is clear that if I have *false beliefs*, I will respond negatively. I cannot help it! Beliefs affect what I say and do. If a man believes that he is stupid, he will act stupidly. If a child believes that she is unloved, she will act out to seek love. If a woman believes that she is trapped in a bad marriage, she might drink or pop pills to escape.

Conversely, if a man believes that he is smart, he will act like he is smart. If a child believes that she is loved by her family, she will not act out to seek love because she already has it. If a woman believes that she has a way to improve her marriage, she will have hope and not turn to alcohol or pills to escape.

The truth is, drugs are not as powerful as they seem. They are not the big, bad, irresistible monsters that we believe them to be. They are inanimate objects! They can do nothing to you on their own. You must *choose* to use and abuse them. However, *beliefs* are *very* powerful. They can cause you to abuse drugs or alcohol. Jesus Christ said:

"There is nothing from without a man, that entering into him can defile him: but the things which come out of him, those are they that defile the man. If any man have ears to hear, let him hear. And when he was entered into the house from the people, his disciples asked him concerning the parable. And he saith unto them, Are ye so without understanding also? Do ye not perceive, that whatsoever thing from without entereth into the man, it cannot defile him; Because it entereth not into his heart, but into the belly, and goeth out into the draught, purging all meats? And he said, That which cometh out of the man, that defileth the man. For from within, out of the heart of men, proceed evil thoughts, adulteries, fornications, murders, Thefts, covetousness, wickedness, deceit, lasciviousness, an evil eye, blasphemy, pride, foolishness: All these evil things come from within, and defile the man." (Mark 7:15-23)

Jesus is talking, here, about food and drink. He says that nothing we put inside of us can defile us. It is what comes out of the heart. The *heart* in the Bible usually refers to the *thoughts, emotions, and will*. Here is an example:

Doug feels trapped in a life of failure. Because of this negative belief, (a belief that comes from his heart: *his thoughts, emotions, and will*), he drinks to get through life and find some relief. Sometimes, he intends to only drink a little but ends up drinking a lot.

It was his job to watch the kids while his wife went to visit her sister. He got drunk and passed out. While it was never his intention to get that drunk, only to drink a little; alcohol and other drugs have a way of distorting our thinking so that we think we need more. In other words, *drugs cause us to use more drugs*. This process takes place when drugs are being used and are influencing our thought processes.

Because Doug (who already believes he is trapped in a life of failure) failed again while watching the children, he feels like even more of a loser than he did before. This causes him to want to drink more to escape from his failure. This is one of the belief patterns of addiction.

Because there are so many false belief patterns associated

with addictive acts, it is important to challenge them with the truth! Jesus prayed, "Sanctify them through thy truth: thy word is truth." (John 17:17) The Word of God is true, and we can challenge false beliefs through Scripture! More about that in the next chapter.

Consequences

There are always consequences to sinful actions. The Bible says, "Be not deceived; God is not mocked: for whatsoever a man soweth, that shall he also reap." (Galatians 6:7) This is an illustration from farming. If we sow corn in the ground, we reap corn. If we sow potatoes, we reap potatoes. It is impossible to sow drunkenness, drug abuse, pornography addiction, or any other sinful thing and not reap negative consequences.

Because of the negative consequences, we see that the sinful act we consented to did not result in *fixing* the problem. It may have put a Band-Aid on it but putting a Band-Aid on a broken leg will not help! You need it set in a cast.

Of course, drinking, drugging; whatever it may be, is just a Band-Aid. It helps you to feel better in the short-term but not in the long-term. You need something bigger and better to fix the problem! We will examine that as we read on.

Benefits Of Using The Abc Chart

Using an ABC Chart, we can not only look at these negative consequences, but also see what triggered the process in the first place, and what false beliefs we had that led us to indulge in that sinful act.

One of the greatest benefits of using an ABC chart is seeing what your false beliefs were in any given circumstance. If you can properly challenge these false beliefs, the next time you face a similar circumstance, you will be prepared to deal with these beliefs before they lead to sinful choices and negative consequences that can mess up your life.

Thought Stopping

You can also use another scientific method to stop yourself before you act on your trigger. It is called "Thought Stopping." Here is how it works: Most people with drug addictions act before they stop and think. The trigger takes place; the thoughts go to using drugs; the drug is used, and consequences occur.

With Thought Stopping, you can tell yourself to "stop!" immediately after the trigger event takes place.[13] Then, you have time to think about what beliefs you are having and whether any of them are false. You can challenge those false beliefs and take positive, rather than negative, action.

5. UNDERSTANDING AND DEALING WITH TRIGGERS FROM A BIBLICAL PERSPECTIVE

Previously, we defined triggers as *events that cause us to want to give in to our addictive behavior*. The reason we define a trigger as an *event* rather than a person, place or thing is because events include people, places, and things in the context of certain specific situations.

For instance: meeting a drug dealer would not make *me* want to buy drugs because I do not use drugs, and have never used drugs (at least, not illegal ones). Therefore, I have no temptation to use drugs. But if a person who is addicted to drugs meets a drug dealer, he or she might be tempted to buy drugs.

You can see from this example how people only become triggers because of the context of the situation. For instance, someone says: "My mother is a trigger for me." Why? What happened in the past or is happening now that makes her a trigger for an addictive response?

Another thing we should look at when examining triggers is the difference between habits and harmful addictions.

Habits

I love coffee. Every morning, before I go to work, I have at least one cup of coffee. One of the most enjoyable experiences when I was a missionary was staying with an older couple in Conyers, Georgia who loved coffee so much that they had, what must have been, a restaurant-grade, industrial coffee maker that brewed coffee constantly. I met my wife during that mission conference and asked her out to get some coffee. Once, when I was preaching in Venezuela and she was living in Peru, I brought down a type of coffee creamer that could not be purchased in South America. I had it sent over to her in Peru. She says that this was one of the reasons she decided to marry me!

Some might say that I am addicted to coffee. However, coffee is really just a habit for me. When I wake up in the morning, I have a strong belief that I *must* have a cup of coffee to be able to properly function. I act on that belief and drink my coffee.

Is my belief true? Not really. I have gone without coffee and was able to carry out my responsibilities without it. However, I enjoy it. It is part of my morning routine. Therefore, I drink coffee and choose to believe that I need it!

What I do not have is *a deep-rooted need* for coffee. In other words, coffee does not meet a complex emotional need. These complex needs are typically present in an addiction.

We often classify things that are just habitual acts as addictions. It becomes more complicated when we add the factor of physical dependency. Am I physically dependent on the drug, caffeine? Probably, since I will eventually get a headache if I do not have any.

This begs another question? Is that really a problem? If I wanted to stop drinking caffeinated drinks, I could just take Tylenol for several days until the physical symptoms passed. The bottom line is I do not have a deep-rooted emotional need for coffee. It is a habit, but not an addiction needing treatment.

The *purpose* of saying all this is to show that not all addictions (habits) need to be treated. My pappy used to sit on his front porch and smoke a cigar every night when the weather was pleasant. I have good memories from that. I have never smoked, and never intend to. But I do not think his smoking was all that harmful. He never developed lung cancer. He did not smoke all the time. It was more of a habit for him.

Simple Triggers

Simple triggers are events that trigger habits and non-complex addictions. For instance, waking up to the belief that I must have coffee to function is my trigger. If I simply change my belief and start having a glass of orange juice every morning, I could stop drinking coffee.

Likewise, the trigger for my pappy's smoking was sitting on his front porch with a cigar. If he had ceased to buy cigars and found something else to do in the evening rather than sitting on the porch, then it is likely that he could have quit smoking.

A man who goes to the local bar every Friday evening to hang out with his friends and ends up drinking too much might be doing this only for social reasons. He enjoys his friends and wants to fit in with the group. If he changed friends and quit going to the bar, he would quit drinking.

Complex Triggers

Unlike simple triggers, complex triggers have a long-term event attached to them. For instance, Susan was molested when she was a child. As an adult, she adopted a child who had been the victim of rape. Susan started smoking cigarettes after adopting the child. She had not smoked since she was in her early 20's and now, she is 35 years old. She cannot figure out why she started smoking again. Her mother died of lung cancer and everyone else in her family has quit smoking.

In this case, the smoking is being used to relieve stress. While being a mother can be very stressful, this stress was *triggered after she adopted the child who had been a victim of rape*. While this would add to the stress of any adoption, it is especially stressful for Susan because it brings up memories of her own victimhood at the hands of a molester.

When Susan thinks about what happened to her adopted child, it causes her to think back to her own experiences which causes her to feel as if she were reliving them again. This makes her feel helpless, which makes her want to smoke. The smoking is something she did as a teenager to defy authority and now it gives her a sense of power over the thoughts, she is having about her victim experience. Plus, the nicotine works chemically as a stress-reliever.

Despite the dangers of smoking, and even though it killed her mother, Susan feels that smoking is the best answer to her pain.

The Burning House

When I was a teenager, I took a mission trip to Mexico. While our team was there, we were working in a village, doing a construction project. Mostly, this consisted of moving cement blocks and working with concrete and stucco. One day, a nearby house caught fire. We rushed to the site. Being an adventurous youth, I decided that I would enter the smoke-filled house to deposit a bucket of water on the fire. Once inside, I discovered that it was dark, and I could not breathe. I rushed back towards the door. Someone was in front of me! I shoved them out of the way and opened the door. At that moment, the only thing that mattered to me was getting oxygen.

A person with a deep-rooted, emotionally based addiction is in a similar situation. Once triggered, the most important thing for them is to get relief by giving in to their temptation. Nothing will stand in their way. This explains why smart and successful people have been known to look at so much pornography at work that they end up losing their jobs. This explains why alcoholics must drink, even when it isn't safe to do so.

"IT DOESN'T REALLY LEAD OUTSIDE."

Addiction compels a person to act. It is like a person who is suffocating, desperately seeking oxygen. Nothing else matters at the time. Most importantly, the addiction is the *answer* to their need. It is the door to get them out of the burning house.

Of course, it doesn't really lead outside, but the addicted person *believes* that it does. That is what matters to them. And as I have said before, what a person *believes* shapes what they think, who they are, and how they act.

Who, What, When, Where, How And Why X 5

To discover what triggered the addictive response and learn what we need to do to have a healthier response in the future, we need to ask some questions. Specifically: *Who, What, When, Where, How and Why (at least five times)*. Here is how this works:

Sam has a very stressful job. Every weekend, he unwinds by using cocaine. He does not use during the week. He goes to work on time and does an efficient job, every day. He hardly ever calls out for any reason. He is a model employee. Yet, his wife and children never enjoy spending time with him on the weekend because he goes into his home office, shuts the door, and gets high. Let's get to the root of Sam's triggers for using cocaine.

> 1. Who? - Sam is obviously involved. So is the drug dealer that he buys the cocaine from (in this case, a friend of his). Also, Sam's boss at work is very demanding and this puts a lot of stress on Sam throughout the week.
> 2. What? - Stress: Sam has a stressful job, brought on mainly by his demanding boss. Sam figures that he

deserves a break on the weekend. What else? Cocaine. Sam uses it to relieve his stress and relax on the weekend.

3. When? - The Weekend: Sam only uses cocaine on the weekend, starting on Saturday. He does this, mainly so that he can spend Friday night watching movies with his children. Saturday is HIS DAY, and so is Sunday!

4. Where? - Obviously, the stressful office environment is one factor. Too, Sam uses the drug in his home office.

5. How? - Sam buys the drug on Friday after work from his friend, who sells it. He always stops by his friend's house before going home.

6. 5 Whys - This system was created by the Toyota Motor Company to determine what was going wrong during the production process. It is helpful in many situations. The idea is to ask "Why?" Five times. By doing this, we can get to the heart of the problem.

    1. Why? Sam uses cocaine on the weekend to unwind from a stressful week at work.

    2. Why? Sam does not like stress because he feels his life is stressful enough without being stressful on the job. He puts pressure on himself to perform. He does not need the added pressure from his boss.

    3. Why? Sam puts pressure on himself to perform because he always has. Even when he was a child, he pressured himself to make straight A's in school to please his father and mother.

    4. Why? Because his father and mother were very demanding. They never seemed satisfied with Sam doing good. He had to be the best! They never were pleased with anything else. One day, he had come home with a B, and his father yelled at him for being a disappointment!

    5. Why? Obviously, his father had some issues that Sam could not understand as a child.

Past & Present: Any Connections?

Now, we will add one more technique that might be helpful at this point. We will ask the question, "Is there a connection between the past and the present situation at Sam's work?"

> 1. PAST - Sam's father and mother were disappointed if he did not make straight A's. This caused Sam to put tremendous pressure on himself to perform which has continued into adulthood.
> 2. PRESENT - Sam's boss pressures him to perform, and Sam pressures himself to perform at work, every day.
> 3. CONNECTIONS? - In both instances, Sam had an authority figure who pressured him to perform and he pressured himself to perform to please the authority figure. Even as an adult, he still feels obligated to perform to please his parents, who are both deceased.

Sam is obviously using cocaine as a means of taking back control of his life, from the *feeling* of being *out of control and trapped* in a hopeless cycle of trying to please authority figures. He dreads the possibility of falling short, of letting the authority figure down. Sam can address and change his faulty beliefs through Bible-based thinking.

It is important to note that your own, "5 Whys" may not take you back to the past, and that is okay.[14] If these help you to understand the series of present-tense events that led to your decision to use, that will be extremely helpful. Ultimately, the goal of using the "5 Whys" is to determine what the *real* issue is: *the reason behind the reason* for your decision to use, and to challenge any false ideas or beliefs.

Thinking Biblically

When I was in Bible College, Dr. Clarence Sexton often said,

"We have to learn to think biblically so that we can know how to think." Biblical thinking is right thinking and can straighten out may false beliefs. The Bible says in the book of Philippians: "Finally, brethren, whatsoever things are true, whatsoever things are honest, whatsoever things are just, whatsoever things are pure, whatsoever things are lovely, whatsoever things are of good report; if there be any virtue, and if there be any praise, think on these things." (Philippians 4:8) Sam could simply follow the first thing on this list and solve his problem with how he responds to pressure: "Whatsoever things are true…think on these things."

1. Is it true that he is obligated to please his parents by doing excellent work at his job? No!

    A. First, his parents are deceased. They no longer care about pressuring him to do a good job. They are probably enjoying heaven, so why should he live under this pressure?

    B. Sam admits that his father and mother had some issues when he was a child that he has never understood. He never pressures his children to get straight A's. Why is he so driven to perform when the people demanding the performance were obviously in the wrong?

    C. Sam is an adult. He has not lived under his parent's roof for years. He took care of them before they died. He has done what a good son should! Why should he continue to live like a child when he is a grown man?

2. Is it true that Sam is obligated to please his demanding boss?

    A. Yes, if he wants to keep his job. However, Sam already does a good job regardless of the pressure his boss puts on him. He does not *need* to perform to please his demanding boss. Here is some more Bible truth: "And whatsoever ye do, do it heartily, as to the Lord, and not unto men;" (Colossians 3:23) When we work a job, our goal should be to work hard and do a good job to please the Lord. We should look beyond our boss, to the Boss of the universe! It is much easier to do a good job for Jesus Christ than for a supervisor with a nasty attitude!

B. Sam is not a slave. He is also not a child, bound to live in his parent's home, by their rules. He can find another job! He is a hard worker, and there is no reason why he should remain in a company where he is constantly harassed by his boss.

By taking these actions, by correcting his false thinking with true, Bible-based thinking, Sam will lose the *need* to use cocaine, and he can finally enjoy the weekends with his family!

More Biblical Thinking

1. *Take positive action, and rest in God's will.*

Before Jesus Christ was arrested, tried and crucified for the sins of the world, the Bible says: "And he went a little further, and fell on his face, and prayed, saying, O my Father, if it be possible, let this cup pass from me: nevertheless not as I will, but as thou wilt." (Matthew 26:39)

The Bible continues, "He went away again the second time, and prayed, saying, O my Father, if this cup may not pass away from me, except I drink it, thy will be done." (Matthew 26:42) Jesus was asking if it was possible, that He might avoid "the cup" of the sufferings of the cross. If not, then He was surrendered to do God's will. He would drink the cup.

You can follow this example. When you are facing a problem, pray for a way out. If God gives you a way, take it. If there is no way, surrender to the will of God. Drink the cup. Get it over with. God will work things out, and His will is better than ours. After all, He has perfect knowledge of all things, and He loves us!

2. *Stay away from things that trigger you.*

God's Word says, "The night is far spent, the day is at hand: let us therefore cast off the works of darkness, and let us put on the armour of light. Let us walk honestly, as in the day; not in rioting and drunkenness, not in chambering and wantonness, not in strife and envying. But put ye on the Lord Jesus Christ, and make not provision for the flesh, to fulfil the lusts thereof." (Romans 13:12-14)

If you have ever been camping, you know that provisions are necessary. These are things that we take to have on hand, in case we need them. The Bible says, "make not provision for the flesh to fulfill the lusts thereof." (V. 14)

Going back to the example of Sam, it is very foolish of him to stop by his friend's house every Friday, since his friend is a drug dealer and Sam has a problem with cocaine! That is making provision for the flesh! "I may need some drugs this weekend. Let me go visit my buddy. He has them if I decide I need them." Says Sam.

If you are addicted to alcohol, don't keep alcohol in your house! If you have a problem with internet pornography, don't have an unfiltered internet connection! Do not make provision for your flesh!

   3. *Look at yourself as God sees you.*

     (1) You are Loved. "Beloved, if God so loved us, we ought also to love one another." (1 John 4:11)

     (2) You are Accepted. "To the praise of the glory of his grace, wherein he hath made us accepted in the beloved." (Ephesians 1:6)

     (3) You are Chosen. "According as he hath chosen us in him before the foundation of the world, that we should be holy and without blame before him in love:" (Ephesians 1:4)

     (4) You have Hope. "That at that time ye were without Christ, being aliens from the commonwealth of Israel, and strangers from the covenants of promise, having no hope, and without God in the world: But now in Christ Jesus ye who sometimes were far off are made nigh by the blood of Christ." (Ephesians 2:12-13)

Change Your Mindset And Change Your Life!

We can use biblical thinking to challenge false beliefs that lead to bad decisions. Through daily reading of the Word of God, our whole mindset will eventually be changed, opening the door to a new way of thinking that aligns with the perfect will of God for us. "And be not conformed to this world: but be ye transformed by the renewing of your mind, that ye may prove what is that good, and acceptable, and perfect, will of God." (Romans 12:2)

6. UNDERSTANDING OUR SIN NATURE.

Everyone who is born in this world is born with something inside that pulls them in the wrong direction. Have you ever noticed it? We often find it easier to do wrong than to do right. The Bible explains this phenomenon as sin: "Wherefore, as by one man sin entered into the world, and death by sin; and so death passed upon all men, for that all have sinned:" (Romans 5:12)

The Bible teaches that sin originally entered the world through the disobedience of a man named Adam. Adam and his wife, Eve, had children. Their first child, Cain, inherited his father's sinful nature. He grew up to be the first murderer in the world! "And Cain talked with Abel his brother: and it came to pass, when they were in the field, that Cain rose up against Abel his brother, and slew him." (Genesis 4:8)

The Bible teaches that all people descend from Adam and Eve. We are all made of one blood. "(God) hath made of one blood all nations of men for to dwell on all the face of the earth, and hath determined the times before appointed, and the bounds of their habitation;" (Acts 17:26)

We inherit our sin nature from Adam, and it causes us to desire to disobey God. Accepting Jesus Christ as Savior changes our lives, but it does not get rid of the sin nature. Sometimes, we will hear a testimony like this: "Before I got saved, I was a drunk. But I came to an altar and repented of my sins and put my faith in Jesus Christ and I haven't touched a drop of alcohol since that day!"

Experiences like this, where all addictions permanently disappear at the moment of salvation, are few and far between. Normally, there is a struggle after salvation. The good news is this: it is a struggle with sin, and sin has been defeated by Jesus Christ on the cross! Therefore, we can have victory through Jesus Christ over our addictions! "But thanks be to God, which giveth us the victory through our Lord Jesus Christ." (1 Corinthians 15:57)

The Nature Of Addiction

The Bible says, "But every man is tempted, when he is drawn away of his own lust, and enticed. Then when lust hath conceived, it bringeth forth sin: and sin, when it is finished, bringeth forth death." (James 1:14-15) As we previously studied, this *lust* inside of us is another word for our *sin nature*. This lust is explained by the Apostle John as part of the driving force behind the Devil's world-system. "For all that is in the world, the lust of the flesh, and the lust of the eyes, and the pride of life, is not of the Father, but is of the world." (1 John 2:16)

Any time that we lust for something sinful, we are doing so because of our sin nature. Is our need to satisfy our addiction a sin? A few things are important to note here:

> 1. Addiction is a result of sin, but the addictive need itself is not sin. Before Adam disobeyed God, there was no addiction. Every aspect of humanity was corrupted by the fall, and therefore, addictions came about. There was never an alcoholic before the fall. There was never a pornography addict before the fall. There was never a pill addict before the fall. There was never a drug dealer before the fall. The fall brought all those things into the world. The important thing to remember is this: it is not a sin for you to have an emotional need for your drug of choice. It is a result of the fall of man. I say that simply because some people believe that they are *awful, terrible, mess-ups* because they struggle with an addiction.

This feeling often leads them to give into their addiction more! Think of how King David dealt with the fact that he had committed adultery and murder.[15] Of course, there were severe consequences. But after he repented, David had to live with what he had done. He said, "Behold, I was shapen in iniquity; and in sin did my mother conceive me." (Psalm 51:5) David remembered his inherited sin nature and accepted the fact that, because he was a sinner, he had done a sinful thing. This acceptance helped him to go on with his life and it can help you too!

2. Temptation is not a sin. It only becomes sin when you give in. "Then when lust hath conceived, it bringeth forth sin: and sin, when it is finished, bringeth forth death." (V. 15)

3. It is a sin when you give in and do something sinful to meet the need of your addiction. The process works, basically like this:

(1) Addiction - a deep-rooted emotional need that we try to satisfy through something harmful.

(2) Temptation - we are tempted by our own sin nature to do something harmful, which we believe will meet the addictive need.

(3) Sin - we give in to the temptation, and sin is the result.

The Struggle With Addiction

It is in the nature of man to struggle. Because our sin nature is not eradicated when we accept Christ as Savior, we will struggle with sin until we die, or the Lord returns. The Apostle Paul described this struggle in Romans, Chapter 7.

"For we know that the law is spiritual: but I am carnal, sold under sin. For that which I do I allow not: for what I would, that do I not; but what I hate, that do I. If then I do that which I would not,

I consent unto the law that it is good. Now then it is no more I that do it, but sin that dwelleth in me. For I know that in me (that is, in my flesh,) dwelleth no good thing: for to will is present with me; but how to perform that which is good I find not. For the good that I would I do not: but the evil which I would not, that I do. Now if I do that I would not, it is no more I that do it, but sin that dwelleth in me. I find then a law, that, when I would do good, evil is present with me. For I delight in the law of God after the inward man: But I see another law in my members, warring against the law of my mind, and bringing me into captivity to the law of sin which is in my members. O wretched man that I am! who shall deliver me from the body of this death? I thank God through Jesus Christ our Lord. So then with the mind I myself serve the law of God; but with the flesh the law of sin." (Romans 7:14-25)

Because the sin nature doesn't go away, you will always struggle with temptation and sin, and so will I. It is completely normal for a person who has an addiction and is in recovery to slip up and fall. That is why you should not be too hard on yourself if you do fall because everyone does. The Bible says, "For a just man falleth seven times, and riseth up again: but the wicked shall fall into mischief." (Proverbs 24:16) If you are a justified (saved) man or woman, you may fall seven times (the number of perfection in the Bible). You may perfectly fall, but it is okay so long as you get back up. It is only shameful if you stay down.

If you are trying to quit drinking or drugging or whatever, and you slip up, get back up and try again! In a boxing match, the boxer is only out if he stays down for the count. Run your race and stay in the fight!

"Wherefore seeing we also are compassed about with so great a cloud of witnesses, let us lay aside every weight, and the sin which doth so easily beset us, and let us run with patience the race that is set before us, Looking unto Jesus the author and finisher of our faith; who for the joy that was set before him endured the cross, despising the shame, and is set down at the right hand of the throne of God." (Hebrews 12:1-2)

In the next several chapters, we will look at four Biblical ideas that will help you to overcome any addiction. The first is *Replacement*.

PART 3. BIBLICAL IDEAS TO DEFEAT ADDICTION

REPLACEMENT; KNOW, RECKON, YIELD; LIFE IN THE SPIRIT, CHRISTIAN FELLOWSHIP

7. UNDERSTANDING THE BIBLICAL IDEA OF REPLACEMENT.

Replacement is an important part of any addiction recovery. The Bible presents this concept in Ephesians, Chapter 4. The Apostle Paul wrote: "Let him that stole steal no more: but rather let him labour, working with his hands the thing which is good, that he may have to give to him that needeth." (Ephesians 4:28)

Several examples of replacement are given in this chapter, but I am going to focus on verse 28. According to God's Word, a man who was a thief should not just quit stealing after he becomes a Christian. He should also replace his stealing with labor.

The Bible is also very specific about the type of labor he should replace his stealing with. It is manual labor, with the hands. Why? Because he used his hands to steal. Now, he is to use his hands for good: to work and make money for himself. He is also to have enough left over to give to others so that they will not steal!

One of my best friends used to be a drug addict and alcoholic. When he got saved, his brother and other young people in the church came to pick him up and bring him to every church meeting. They took him out to eat. They created reasons to hang out with him. He told me that if they had not done this, he would have just gone back to hanging out with his friends who used drugs and would have returned to drugs and alcohol. Replacement is so important!

An Evil Spirit And An Empty House

Jesus told the story of a man who had an evil spirit in his house. He said: "When the unclean spirit is gone out of a man, he walketh through dry places, seeking rest; and finding none, he saith, I will return unto my house whence I came out. And when he cometh, he findeth it swept and garnished. Then goeth he, and taketh to him seven other spirits more wicked than himself; and they enter in, and dwell there: and the last state of that man is worse than the first." (Luke 11:24-26)

In this case, the man got rid of the evil and cleaned up his house. But he did not replace the evil with something good. He did not ask Jesus Christ to come in. Therefore, the evil spirit went off and could not find another place to live. He stopped back by the man's house where he was evicted and saw that it was empty. So, he got some of his friends and said, "Hey! I know where we can go! We'll move in with this guy I used to live with!" They went to his house and because it was clean, but not filled with God, they moved in and the man was worse off in the end than he was at the beginning.

This is why we need to fill our lives with something positive when we take drugs and alcohol away. If we do not, our addictions may come back with a vengeance! If you used to drink alcohol with friends at the pub, you may find it helpful to hang out with friends from church at a coffee shop instead. If you typically keep a pack of cigarettes in your shirt pocket, you may find it helpful to keep a small New Testament in your shirt pocket. Then, when you reach for your cigarettes, you have something positive to replace them.

Replace Negativity With Positive Self-Talk.

For example: if you tell yourself that you are in an *awful* situation that can *only* be solved by escaping with drugs, practice telling yourself instead that you *may* be in a *bad* situation, but not an awful or hopeless one. Quote hopeful Bible verses to yourself. For example:

"To the chief Musician, A Psalm of David. I waited patiently for the LORD; and he inclined unto me, and heard my cry. He brought me up also out of an horrible pit, out of the miry clay, and set my feet upon a rock, and established my goings. And he hath put a new song in my mouth, even praise unto our God: many shall see it, and fear, and shall trust in the LORD." (Psalms 40:1-3)

"For God hath not given us the spirit of fear; but of power, and of love, and of a sound mind." (2 Timothy 1:7)

"Brethren, I count not myself to have apprehended: but this one thing I do, forgetting those things which are behind, and reaching forth unto those things which are before, I press toward the mark for the prize of the high calling of God in Christ Jesus." (Philippians 3:13-14)

Encourage yourself in the Lord! If you change your speech you can change your thinking. If you change your thinking, you can change your whole belief system!

Replace Bitterness With Forgiveness.

The Bible says, "Let all bitterness, and wrath, and anger, and clamour, and evil speaking, be put away from you, with all malice: And be ye kind one to another, tenderhearted, forgiving one another, even as God for Christ's sake hath forgiven you." (Ephesians 4:31-32)

You may feel trapped in a relationship where there is constant yelling, fussing, cussing, arguing, etc. The Bible tells us to put these things away: get rid of them. But we are to replace them with kindness and forgiveness. When we speak kind words to our loved ones, it will bring peace to the home. "A soft answer turneth away wrath: but grievous words stir up anger." (Proverbs 15:1)

Forgiveness is possible because God has forgiven us for Jesus

Christ's sake. When Christ died on the cross, he paid the price for all of our sins and all of the sins of everyone who has ever wronged us. Just as God forgives you based on the substitutionary death of Jesus Christ, you can forgive others based on this same substitution. "Jesus paid for your sins and wants me to forgive you, therefore I forgive you." There is no need for sin to be paid for twice!

Perhaps your mother was not there for you as a child. You have never forgiven her for that. Forgive her now, for Christ. You may not be able to forgive her for her. But Jesus is your Lord and Savior. Forgive her for Him!

To *forgive* does not mean to *forget* as we are often taught. We can't forget things that were done in the past. Forgiveness means *to release a person from owing you a debt.* When we live our lives with people on the hook for debts we believe they owe because of wrongs done to us in the past, then every time they do something again, we just add it to the list of wrongs, and the debt grows.

By forgiving the person who has wronged you, you are simply deciding that they no longer owe you. You have released them from their debt to you because Jesus Christ has already paid the price for their sins. By releasing this person, you can have the possibility of a new and better relationship with him or her, if that is something that you want.

Replace Controlling Situations With Freedom In Christ.

The Bible says, "Stand fast therefore in the liberty wherewith Christ hath made us free, and be not entangled again with the yoke of bondage." (Galatians 5:1)

If you are in a church that tries to control you and your family; telling you what kind of car to buy, house to live in, how many children to have, and dozens of other things that are none of their concern, then get out! Jesus said, "...Ye know that the princes of the Gentiles exercise dominion over them, and they that are great exercise authority upon them. But it shall not be so among you: but whosoever will be great among you, let him be your minister; And whosoever will be chief among you, let him be your servant: Even as the Son of man came not to be ministered unto, but to minister, and to give his life a ransom for many. " (Matthew 20:25-28)

If you are in an abusive marriage, get help, and get things changed, or leave. Even if you do not believe in divorce, you can still leave the situation without divorcing. You do not have to live under abuse! Someone might ask, "But doesn't the Bible teach that women should obey their husbands and submit themselves?" Certainly, it does: "Wives, submit yourselves unto your own husbands, as unto the Lord. For the husband is the head of the wife, even as Christ is the head of the church: and he is the saviour of the body. Therefore as the church is subject unto Christ, so let the wives be to their own husbands in every thing." (Ephesians 5:22-24)

However, the Bible also teaches that husbands are to submit to their wives through sacrificial love. "Husbands, love your wives, even as Christ also loved the church, and gave himself for it; That he might sanctify and cleanse it with the washing of water by the word, That he might present it to himself a glorious church, not having spot, or wrinkle, or any such thing; but that it should be holy and without blemish. So ought men to love their wives as their own bodies. He that loveth his wife loveth himself." (Ephesians 5:25-28)

How anyone could interpret these Scriptures to teach that husbands have the right to physically and verbally *abuse* and *control* their wives and that their wives have to *submit* to that, is beyond me! The Bible teaches that a loving, Spirit-filled home relationship is characterized by mutual submission: wives obeying their husbands who sacrifice their own wants and needs to please the wife. Both are submitting to one another and trying to please each other. Distortions of this Scripture which focus solely on the wife's duty have caused some "Christian" abusers to be able to get away with unspeakable things.

Remember, that we have previously stated that people use addictions to gain a sense of control in their lives. By taking actual control of a situation, you will replace the need for the drug/alcohol/pornography/gambling. You will replace your addiction of choice with real freedom in obedience to Scripture!

Replace Your Past With A Bright Future.

The Apostle Paul wrote: "Brethren, I count not myself to have apprehended: but this one thing I do, forgetting those things which are behind, and reaching forth unto those things which are before, I press toward the mark for the prize of the high calling of God in Christ Jesus." (Philippians 3:13-14)

Paul had been a persecutor of Christians before he got saved. He hunted believers down and had them jailed, tortured, and killed.[16] How did he deal with his past? He did not focus on it. He dismissed the things that were in the past and focused on his goals for the future. His goal was Jesus Christ, and he focused on Him.

You do not have to stay stuck in the past. You can change things. Take action! Change your future by changing your present. Several years ago, I was very depressed and felt stuck in a bad situation. One day I thought, "What would I do if I were living in another place and under different circumstances?" I imagined what I would do if that were the case, so I decided to try to do it where I was. Within a few months, my entire life had changed for the better! Do not stay stuck in the past. Press forward!

Replace Your Worries About The Future With Prayer.

The Bible says, "Be careful for nothing; but in every thing by prayer and supplication with thanksgiving let your requests be made known unto God. And the peace of God, which passeth all understanding, shall keep your hearts and minds through Christ

Jesus." (Philippians 4:6-7)

Paul writes, "Don't worry about anything. Do not be filled with care." How do we quit worrying? We pray. "...But in every thing by prayer and supplication with thanksgiving let your requests be made known unto God." (V. 6) With prayer, I can overcome worry because I transfer the burden of solving problems from myself to Almighty God. I stop trying to fix things and start trusting in God's plan, timing, and will.

The Bible says, "And the peace of God, which passeth all understanding, shall keep your hearts and minds through Christ Jesus." (V. 7) The word translated, "keep" in this verse means *to guard, like a military garrison*. When we pray, the peace of God will stand guard before us. The phrase, "shall keep" is in the future tense. Most of what we worry about is in the future. These are things that we cannot do anything about because they have not happened yet. But when we pray about them, God gives his peace to guard our hearts and minds. With God, we will be prepared for the future; not filled with worry and uncertainty.

Plans For Change

If you are feeling stuck, here is a simple tool you can use to plan a new and better future. Take a piece of paper and write down something you would like to change in your life. Write down, specifically, how you will make this change and any obstacles you think will stand in your way. Then, write down ways to overcome the obstacles. Find some people that can help you make this happen; then, act on it!

Your life does not have to stay stuck in an addictive pattern. You can change, but not without replacement. By replacing negative thoughts, choices, and situations with those that are positive, you can change your life for the better!

Now, we will examine a second Biblical idea that will help you to overcome addiction. It is the concept of *Know, Reckon, and Yield*.

8. UNDERSTANDING HOW TO KNOW, RECKON, AND YIELD.

Imagine the scene. A battle is about to take place. An old man is getting ready to unite with a vicious monster called sin and attack you. He intends to persuade you to give your body over to drugs, drinking, sexual immorality, and much more. What can you do to stop him before sin invades and reigns over you? Read further and find out! The old man is a reality in the life of every believer. It is important to know your enemy, so we will begin with that.

We Need To Know.

"Knowing this, that our old man is crucified with him, that the body of sin might be destroyed, that henceforth we should not serve sin." (Romans 6:6)

Our "old man" is our old life of sin. When Jesus Christ died on the cross, He died for our sins-each and every one. Therefore, "our old man was crucified with him." This happened so that "the body of sin might be destroyed." The word translated, "destroyed" means, "rendered inoperative." Our old life of sin, which was lived in the human body, has been rendered inoperative. It is like a car with no tires or motor. It is still a car, but it cannot go anywhere. We need to know that the old life we lived, and whatever addiction it included, has been crucified with Christ on the cross. The body of sin has been destroyed.

When Jesus was hanging on the cross, dying for the sins of the world, the Bible tells us that there were two criminals crucified with Him. One was on His right, and the other on His left. The Bible says, "And one of the malefactors which were hanged railed on him, saying, If thou be Christ, save thyself and us. But the other answering rebuked him, saying, Dost not thou fear God, seeing thou art in the same condemnation?" (Luke 23:39-40)

At first, God's Word tells us that both criminals, who were dying with Jesus, made fun of Him. However, as death progressed, one of the criminals changed his attitude and decided that Jesus Christ was the Son of God: "And he said unto Jesus, Lord, remember me when thou comest into thy kingdom. And Jesus said unto him, Verily I say unto thee, To day shalt thou be with me in paradise." (Luke 23:42-43)

However, the other criminal continued to refuse to believe that Jesus was the Savior. He continued to mock Him. Let us focus on that criminal because he is very much like the old man. Romans 6:6 says, "Knowing this, that our old man is crucified with him..." Our old life is like the dying thief. He has been rendered inoperative because he is dying on the cross. He is powerless to do anything but talk. And he talks and mocks and says: "You are such a loser. Why don't you go get drunk! You are stuck in this situation. There is no way out. Go get high! Your spouse doesn't appreciate you. You are trapped in a dead-end marriage. Look at pornography!"

Sometimes, we resist the old man. Sometimes, we listen to him and believe him. But we need to know that he is not what he used to be. He has lost his power because he is crucified. Therefore, he cannot make you do anything. He can only talk and try to persuade you to give in to sin.

We Need To Reckon.

"Likewise reckon ye also yourselves to be dead indeed unto sin, but alive unto God through Jesus Christ our Lord." (Romans 6:11)

You must "reckon" which means, "count it true for yourself" that you are indeed dead to sin, but alive to God through Jesus Christ. It is not enough for you to know that the old life is crucified, but you must act and live as if it is crucified. How do you do this?

We Need To Yield.

"Let not sin therefore reign in your mortal body, that ye should obey it in the lusts thereof." (Romans 6:12)

You do not have to let sin rule in your body by obeying its demands. You do not have to obey the urge to get drunk, high, or whatever your addiction of choice may be. You do not have to let sin reign! Sin is like a failed despot who comes to a free man or woman shouting: "Obey me! I am your master!" In fact, sin is a failed ruler who no longer reigns over our lives because Jesus Christ is on the throne! The Bible goes on to say,

"Neither yield ye your members as instruments of unrighteousness unto sin: but yield yourselves unto God, as those that are alive from the dead, and your members as instruments of righteousness unto God." (Romans 6:13)

We carry out our resistance to sin by simply refusing to yield our hands, feet, eyes, mouth, ears, and bodies as weapons ("instruments" means instruments of war) for sin's use. We also practice replacement, which we discussed in the last chapter. We yield ourselves to God as free people, alive from the dead, and we yield our members (body parts) as instruments of warfare to be used for righteousness. Instead of fighting against ourselves by abusing drugs and alcohol, we fight the Devil by spreading the Gospel and loving one another.

"For sin shall not have dominion over you: for ye are not under the law, but under grace." (Romans 6:14)

Finally, sin will not rule over us. We are not under the Old Testament law. We are under grace-the undeserved, unearned favor of God. It is under the banner of God's grace that we will find victory over addiction!

In the next chapter, we will examine a third Biblical concept to overcome addiction: Life in the Spirit.

9. UNDERSTANDING LIFE IN THE SPIRIT.

Addiction rehab facilities are helpful to many people. They are especially good for detox, which allows addicts to safely come off drugs or alcohol. However, rehab usually lasts anywhere from 45 days to 6 months. Once it is over and the recovering user returns to the outside world, he or she has to be prepared to maintain recovery.

The Bible, on the other hand, gives us a tool that works for the rest of our lives. It is a safe place we can live no matter where we are. It is life in the Spirit. The Bible says: "This I say then, Walk in the Spirit, and ye shall not fulfil the lust of the flesh. For the flesh lusteth against the Spirit, and the Spirit against the flesh: and these are contrary the one to the other: so that ye cannot do the things that ye would." (Galatians 5:16-17)

In this Scripture, *the Spirit* is the Holy Spirit of God. *The flesh* is the old man that we studied in the last chapter. Another name for the flesh is our *sin nature* or *the life of sin we lived before salvation*. The Bible teaches that the "flesh lusts against the Spirit and the Spirit against the flesh." (V. 17) In other words, there is a constant struggle. The Holy Spirit wants you to live a good life that pleases God, and the flesh (the old man) wants you to give in to temptation and sin.

Walking In The Spirit

The Bible tells us that if we, "walk in the Spirit" we will "not fulfill the lusts of the flesh." (V. 16) To "walk in the Spirit" means to live our lives in the Spirit. Before salvation, we lived in the flesh. In that place, we gave in to our addiction. Now, we have moved to a new residence. It is life in the Spirit! If we live life in the power of the Holy Spirit and take advantage of the things God has for us in this new life, we will not act on the temptations that the flesh brings us.

Living Under Grace

The Bible goes on to say, "But if ye be led of the Spirit, ye are not under the law." (Galatians 5:18) Thank God, we are not under the law. We are under grace! Living under the law is living under a system that says, "Either do this or you will die! If you want to live, obey these rules."

"For Moses describeth the righteousness which is of the law, That the man which doeth those things shall live by them." (Romans 10:5)

Grace is not like that. Grace says, "You have life. Now, live for God; not to gain salvation, but because you already have it." Grace does not give us a set of rules to follow but introduces us to life led by the Holy Spirit of God. "But if ye be led of the Spirit, ye are not under the law." (V. 18)

Unfortunately, forced rehab or court-ordered counseling are often unsuccessful in the long run. Why? Because they are based on the law rather than grace. A person is not choosing to get better because they want to. They are forced to get better to avoid more jail time. I cannot count the number of teenagers who have told me, "I'm going to stay off of drugs until I am off probation." That is the way the law works. It says, "Obey and you will have freedom." Grace, on the other hand, says: "Have freedom so that you can obey!"

The Works Of The Flesh

The Bible also describes the works of the flesh. "Now the works of the flesh are manifest, which are these; Adultery, fornication, uncleanness, lasciviousness, Idolatry, witchcraft, hatred, variance, emulations, wrath, strife, seditions, heresies, Envyings, murders, drunkenness, revellings, and such like: of the which I tell you before, as I have also told you in time past, that they which do such things shall not inherit the kingdom of God." (Galatians 5:19-21)

These evil works include drunkenness, drug use, sexual immorality, and many other things. We would recognize some of these as addictions. Contrast that with the new life we have in the Spirit. "But the fruit of the Spirit is love, joy, peace, longsuffering, gentleness, goodness, faith, Meekness, temperance: against such there is no law." (Galatians 5:22-23)

You will never get in trouble for living life in the Spirit because there is no law against any of these things. Compare that to things done in the flesh. Not only is God's law against all of them, but man's laws are against some as well.

A Decision You Must Make

The Bible says, "And they that are Christ's have crucified the flesh with the affections and lusts. If we live in the Spirit, let us also walk in the Spirit." (Galatians 5:24-25) If you belong to Jesus Christ; the old man, the flesh, has been crucified. He is nailed to the cross, unable to exercise power over you. But as we learned in the last chapter, he can run his mouth and try to trick you into giving into sin.

That is why we have to decide to walk in the Spirit. In verse 25, the Bible says, "If we live in the Spirit, let us also walk in the Spirit." When you got saved, you changed addresses, spiritually. It would be like a man who moved from an old, dirty, one-room apartment to a nice, clean, spacious mansion. He has everything he needs in the mansion, but sometimes he longs for the old life. Instead of walking in the mansion where he lives, he goes back to the old, dirty apartment and walks there. He smokes the dope, drinks the liquor, and lives like a lost man, even though he is saved and has a new home in the Spirit.

All believers live in the Spirit, but not all believers *walk* in the Spirit. How do we walk in the Spirit? We choose to live our lives, led by the Holy Spirit, in "love, joy, peace, longsuffering, gentleness, goodness, faith, Meekness, temperance." (Galatians 5:22-23) These things are the "fruit of the Spirit" according to verse 22, so they are a natural result of walking in the Spirit.

The Bible describes the believer who is walking with God in this way: "And he shall be like a tree planted by the rivers of water, that bringeth forth his fruit in his season; his leaf also shall not wither; and whatsoever he doeth shall prosper." (Psalm 1:3)

As we follow the Spirit's leading, we will walk in the Spirit. As we walk in the Spirit, we will be like a tree that brings forth good fruit. We will produce good works and live a peaceful and joyful life. If you are stuck in a pattern from your old life, maybe it is because you are walking in the flesh instead of in the Spirit!

A Daily Walk

Finally, what practical things can we do every day to walk in the Spirit? The answer is simple: read the Bible and pray daily. Pick a book of the Bible to begin with, (Matthew, Mark, Luke, or John would be best) and then read and obey. Remember that James says, "But be ye doers of the word, and not hearers only, deceiving your own selves." (James 1:22)

As we read and attempt to obey the Bible, we should pray about our needs. As we do this, the Spirit of God will lead us. He can show us, through His Word, how to forgive, treat our enemies, get our prayers answered, have faith when things look hopeless, etc.

As the Spirit leads us, we will produce the fruit of the Spirit. As we do, we will not fulfill the lusts of the flesh because we will have replaced the old, sinful lifestyle of addiction with a new, joyful lifestyle of following God!

"This I say then, Walk in the Spirit, and ye shall not fulfil the lust of the flesh." (Galatians 5:16)

Another important part of walking in the Spirit is having regular, Christian fellowship by attending church. We will take a look at that in the next chapter.

10. UNDERSTANDING THE IMPORTANCE OF CHRISTIAN FELLOWSHIP.

One of the most important things you can do to maintain your recovery is to get involved in a local church, an assembly of believers who can encourage one another and hold one another accountable.

According to a 2018 article published in *Military Medicine* by Tyler J. VanderWeele, attendance of religious services has many benefits, including reducing rates of substance abuse.

> Over the past couple of decades, a large body of research has emerged suggesting that religious participation is strongly associated with numerous health and well-being outcomes. Large well-designed research studies have indicated that religious service attendance is associated with greater longevity, less depression, less suicide, less smoking, less substance abuse, better cancer and cardiovascular disease survival, less divorce, greater social support, greater meaning and purpose in life, greater life satisfaction, more charitable giving, more volunteering, and greater civic engagement.[17]

The Founder Of The Church

Jesus Christ started the church and gave His life for it.

"And I say also unto thee, That thou art Peter, and upon this rock I will build my church; and the gates of hell shall not prevail against it." (Matthew 16:18) Jesus told Peter (whose name meant, *a stone*) that He would build His church upon something big: *"this rock."* The "rock" did not refer to Peter, but to Christ Himself. The Bible teaches that Jesus Christ is the chief cornerstone of the church.

"Now therefore ye are no more strangers and foreigners, but fellowcitizens with the saints, and of the household of God; And are built upon the foundation of the apostles and prophets, Jesus Christ himself being the chief corner stone." (Ephesians 2:19-20)

The Bible teaches that Christ loved the church and gave His life for it. "Husbands, love your wives, even as Christ also loved the church, and gave himself for it;" (Ephesians 5:25)

If the church is important enough for Jesus Christ to start, build and give His life for, we need to attend it!

We Need Fellowship.

Church attendance is very important! You cannot grow as a believer without Christian fellowship and encouragement. As Pastor Wayne Cofield says,

> Church membership is important because church membership is identifying with God's family. When you join a team, you are not supposed to be ashamed of it! That is why you need to fellowship and be trained in the local church and be accountable to the local church. That is why you ought to join a church that believes the Bible and preaches the Bible. You can be accountable in that church. Also, the fellowship will encourage you. If you set a piece of charcoal by itself, it will cool off. But, if you put that piece of charcoal with other pieces of charcoal, it will stay warm and glowing![18]

Try to find a good, Bible-believing church that preaches and teaches salvation by grace through faith, believer's baptism, and that believes in teaching the Bible verse by verse, in an expository manner.

Those Who Won't Attend.

Ever since the church began, there have been Christians who have downplayed the importance of church attendance. The Bible says, "Not forsaking the assembling of ourselves together, as the manner of some is; but exhorting one another: and so much the more, as ye see the day approaching." (Hebrews 10:25)

There are always *some* who say, "We don't need to go to church. We can worship just fine in the woods on Sunday or on the lake with a fishing rod, beer cooler, and boat." But the author of Hebrews warns us that we should not "forsake the assembling of ourselves together." (V. 25) Church attendance is essential to a Christian's spiritual growth.

Use Caution.

In some modern churches, it has become popular for small group leaders and members to drink alcohol during the group meeting time. Some even meet in pubs. While this may surprise you, do not put yourself in danger by joining a small group where the leader drinks. "Craft beer" might be a fun thing for some, but for a recovering alcoholic, it could be a disaster! Abstinence is always the best policy when you have issues with drug or alcohol dependency and are trying to recover.

Any new Christian should use caution when choosing a place to grow and worship. Be picky about doctrine. Do not go to a church that tries to control every aspect of your life. Stay away from churches that do not follow the Bible as their only source of faith and doctrine.

Sometimes large churches are better and sometimes small churches are better. It depends on where you fit best. Find a place where you can serve God, worship with your family, and get involved in the church!

11. CLOSING THOUGHTS.

It is important to summarize all the information that we have read and try to memorize it and put it into practice. Like anything else, reading information will not help half as much as memorization and practice. After all, "Practice makes perfect." Here is a summary of the most important concepts in this book:

ADDICTION is not as powerful as it seems. You can overcome addiction, temptation, and your drug of choice through the power of God and your own will. You are not powerless over an addiction! Read about this in Chapter 2.

ADDICTION involves deception. Recognize the tricks that your mind will play on you to try to get you to yield to your temptation. Challenge these false beliefs with the truth! See Chapter 3 for more.

ADDICTION can be analyzed and defeated by using the ABC Chart method, presented in Chapter 4 of this book.

ADDICTION is triggered by certain events but you can analyze and defeat these triggers before they trip you up! See Chapter 5.

ADDICTION is a result of the sin nature that we inherit from Adam. Because we are all sinners, we will fall; but we can rise up and try again! We do not have to be defeated. See Chapter 6.

ADDICTION can be defeated by using the Bible's idea of Replacement. See Chapter 7.

ADDICTION can be defeated using the Bible formula of Know, Reckon, and Yield. See Chapter 8.

ADDICTION and recovery can be managed in the long run by living life in the Spirit. Learn about this in Chapter 9.

ADDICTION and recovery can be managed by spending time with other believers who can encourage you in the church. See Chapter 10.

Here are some additional resources that you can use to help with addiction.

Books:

The Heart of Addiction: *A New Approach to Understanding and Managing Alcoholism and Other Addictive Behaviors* by Lance Dodes, M.D.
ISBN-10 : 0060958030
ISBN-13 : 978-0060958039

Breaking Addiction: *A 7-Step Handbook for Ending Any Addiction* by Lance Dodes, M.D.
ISBN-10 : 0061987395
ISBN-13 : 978-0061987397

Web:

https://www.smartrecovery.org

https://findtreatment.gov

ABOUT THE AUTHOR

STEPHEN BAKER is the author of nine books and various Bible studies.

Trained by the Georgia Department of Juvenile Justice in the use of Cognitive Behavioral Therapy for group counseling.

Certified as a SMART Recovery® group facilitator and trained in Rational Emotive Behavioral Therapy.

Experienced in the use of 7 Challenges Brief® curriculum for individual substance abuse counseling.

Stephen has counseled incarcerated teens since 2013. He works professionally as a Juvenile Detention Counselor and Case Manager.

Stephen earned his Master's Degree in Ministry from Crown College in Powell, Tennessee and has over twenty years of ministry and pastoral counseling experience.

Stephen served as a foreign missionary for five years with Macedonia World Baptist Missions.

He currently serves God as the Pastor of a small Baptist

congregation in Dalton, Georgia.

Stephen is married to April. The Bakers have two children, two dogs and two cats.

BIBLIOGRAPHY

1. Cofield, Kenneth W. "The Real Life: Chapter 3: Join the Church." Grow Strong: Basic Building Blocks For Becoming a Strong Christian, edited by Stephen D Baker, CrossLife Press, 2015, pp. 16–16.
2. Dodes, Lance. The Heart of Addiction. Harper, 2002, Apple Books. , books.apple.com/us/book/the-heart-of-addiction/id373351516.
3. National Institute on Drug Abuse. "Drugs and the Brain." National Institute on Drug Abuse, 10 July 2020, www.drugabuse.gov/publications/drugs-brains-behavior-science-addiction/drugs-brain.
4. Spirit, Holy. The Holy Bible, Containing the Old and New Testaments, Translated out of the Original Tongues, and with the Former Translations Diligently Compared and Revised: Authorized King James Version. Thomas Nelson, 2017.
5. Strong, James. Strong's Exhaustive Concordance to the Bible. Hendrickson Pub, 2009.
6. Thayer, Joseph Henry, et al. Thayer's Greek-English Lexicon of the New Testament: Coded with Strong's Concordance Numbers. Hendrickson, 2017.
7. VanderWeele, Tyler J. "Religious Communities, Health, and Well-Being – Address to the US Air Force Chaplain." OUP Academic, Oxford University Press, 23 Mar. 2018, doi.org/10.1093/milmed/usx206.

---

[1] CBT focuses on the present instead of the past and attempts to change

a person's actions by changing his or her thinking. This harmonizes with the Biblical idea of repentance.

[2] They may not lose much of anything. They may be "high-functioning" users, holding down a steady job and taking care of their family. Yet, the pattern is the same: they cannot seem to quit no matter what the risks and potential costs are.

[3] Thayer's Greek Lexicon G4851 Def. 2C.

[4] Strong's Concordance G1850 Def.

[5] Excerpt From: Lance M. Dodes, M.D. "The Heart of Addiction." Apple Books. https://books.apple.com/us/book/the-heart-of-addiction/id373351516

[6] Ibid.

[7] Of course, a person might not want the addiction and bad effects of a drug yet want the good feelings that it causes.

[8] See Chapter 4 on "Thought Stopping."

[9] See Chapter 5 on "Habits."

[10] https://www.drugabuse.gov/publications/drugs-brains-behavior-science-addiction/drugs-brain

[11] Thayer's Greek Lexicon G1828 Def. 2.

[12] The ABC Chart comes from Rational Emotive Behavioral Therapy which, like CBT, does not focus on the past. However, therapists like Dr. Lance Dodes believe that the past is essential to solving addictions. I take an approach in this book of combining both methods.

[13] You can practice this by visualizing something that makes you think of stopping, like a stop sign or slamming on the brakes. Practice doing this over and over again.

[14] Sometimes, thinking back to past events can itself be a trigger for an addictive action. Therefore, it may be healthier for you to concentrate only on the events leading up to your decision in the present. Also, if you want to work on past traumatic events, seeing a licensed psychotherapist may be helpful.

[15] See Ch. 4

[16] Was Paul like a terrorist? More like a Nazi Gestapo agent. What he did was completely legal, but evil.

[17] Tyler J VanderWeele, Religious Communities, Health, and Well-Being – Address to the US Air Force Chaplain, Military Medicine, Volume 183, Issue 5-6, May-June 2018, Pages 105–109, https://doi.org/10.1093/milmed/usx206

[18] From Grow Strong: Basic Building Blocks for Becoming a Strong Christian, By Cofield & Baker. Pg. 16.

BOOKS BY THIS AUTHOR

Grow Strong: Basic Building Blocks For Becoming A Strong Christian

Grow Strong: Basic Building Blocks for Becoming a Strong Christian is two books in one. The first, The Real Life by Pastor Wayne Cofield, is written for new Christians. It is about taking the first steps in the Christian life. It includes seven short studies, memory verses and a study guide to help the new believer set out in the right direction on his or her journey of faith. The second book, Relationship and Fellowship by Pastor Stephen Baker, contains an in-depth study of salvation and assurance. It gives some of the basic building blocks that new believers and old alike will need for successful Christian living. It includes ten chapters on subjects like assurance of salvation, how to overcome sin, Bible study methods and more!

Raised: A Story Of Salvation

Benjamin Lazarus works as a telemarketer, selling overpriced timeshares to unwary, elderly victims. He is the best employee at the company, because he can lie like no one else. On a stormy Monday morning, he is about to discover a secret. He is, in reality, dead. An expert team of villains follow Benjamin and try to trip him up at every turn on his quest to get out of the grave. But there are other forces at work in his life. Benjamin has a caring Uncle and a loving God who are intent on seeing him live.

Relationship And Fellowship

Relationship and Fellowship is a book about knowing that you are saved and living for Jesus Christ after salvation. "After struggling with assurance of my own salvation for years and finally getting the victory, I can show you clearly, from the Word of God, how to be sure that you will go to Heaven when you die. As a pastor and minister of the Gospel, this book contains Biblical lessons I have learned about living for Jesus Christ." -Stephen Baker

Hope: God's Shelter In The Storms Of Life

Need some encouragement? Having all the problems that you can handle? This book will show you Bible truths about the radical hope that God offers to you through Jesus Christ. HOPE covers such topics as: How to overcome depression, the meaning of Romans 8:28, The testimony of a convicted drug dealer and gang member who found hope in Jesus Christ, and much more!

How We Got The English Bible

In HOW WE GOT THE ENGLISH BIBLE, you will read the amazing story of how God's Word originally came to man, how it was preserved over the centuries, and how it has been translated into the English language.

LEGAL THINGS YOU SHOULD KNOW.

There are stories in this book that are provided for illustration purposes. They are wholly fictitious, and any names, characters, events or incidents are the product of the author's imagination. Any resemblance to actual persons, living or dead, or actual events is purely coincidental.

The content of this book is for informational purposes only and is not intended to diagnose, treat, cure, or prevent any condition or disease. You understand that this book is not intended as a substitute for consultation with a licensed practitioner. Please consult with your own physician, counselor or healthcare specialist regarding the suggestions and recommendations made in this book. The author and publisher expressly disclaim responsibility for any adverse effects arising from the use or application of the information contained herein. The use of this book implies your acceptance of this disclaimer.

Made in the USA
Columbia, SC
12 October 2024